4

D0855915

Best Poems of 1975

Best Poems of 1975
Borestone Mountain Poetry Awards 1976

A Compilation of Original Poetry
Published in Magazines of the
English-Speaking World in 1975

Volume 28

Pacific Books, Publishers, Palo Alto, California
1976

International Standard Book Number 0-87015-223-8.
Library of Congress Catalog Card Number 49-49262.
Printed and bound in the United States of America.

PACIFIC BOOKS, PUBLISHERS
P.O. Box 558, Palo Alto, California 94302

FOREWORD

Best Poems of 1975 presents the Borestone Mountain Poetry Awards' twenty-eighth annual selections of poems from magazines of the English-speaking world issued in 1975. The selections are poems of not more than one hundred lines first printed in 1975. No reprints or translations are considered, and poems are not solicited or accepted directly from the poets. The reading staff and editors, working independently of one another, select from assigned magazines the poems they believe to be the most outstanding. In this way some three hundred poems are selected by the end of the year and approximately one hundred and fifty magazines covered in the English-speaking world.

When the year's selections are complete, copies of the poems are sent to the editors serving as judges with the names of the authors and magazines deleted, as there is no intention of recognizing established names in preference to newcomers or apportioning selections between magazines and countries. The judges score their top seventy-five individual preferences and forward the results to the office of the Managing Editor, where a tabulation of the scores determines the final selections. The three highest scores are the winners of the year's cash awards. Because of the anonymity preserved during the selection process, the final results may include more than one poem by a poet and a number of poems from the same periodical.

Borestone Mountain Poetry Awards, which was established thirty years ago, is supported by a not-for-profit literary foundation by the same name. The purpose is to preserve in book form each year some of the poems of merit that otherwise might be lost among countless magazine pages. The twenty-eight annual volumes have presented more than 2,100 poems by more than 1,000 contemporary poets, and the series now serves as an easy and useful reference to some of the best writing in contemporary poetry during the past three decades.

"Lot: Some Speculations" by Jon Dressel received the first award of $300. "Clancy" by David Wagoner, "How It Is" by Maxine Kumin, and "A Mountain Lion" by Ted Hughes tied for the second award and each poet received $200.

The editors gratefully acknowledge permission to reprint these selected poems from the magazines, publishers, and authors owning the copyrights. Listed in the Contents are the magazines and issue in 1975 from which the selection was made. At the time the selections were completed in April 1975, some poems were scheduled for reprinting in collections of the poets. These subsequent printings and other recognitions are recorded under Acknowledgments and Notes.

THE EDITORS

HOWARD SERGEANT
*British Commonwealth
Magazines
(except Canada)*

WADDELL AUSTIN
Managing Editor

HILDEGARDE FLANNER

FRANCES MINTURN HOWARD

GEMMA D'AURIA

GARY MIRANDA

ACKNOWLEDGMENTS AND NOTES

"Walking Out" by Betty Adcock was selected from the original printing in *North Carolina: The Seventies, a Special Issue of Southern Poetry Review, Vol. XV.* The poem was included in her first book of poems, *Walking Out* © 1975 Betty Adcock, which was published by Louisiana State University Press in November 1975. The poem is reprinted by permission of the author and Louisiana State University Press.

"Absolute Clearance" is also from the collection of poems *Self-Portrait in a Convex Mirror* by John Ashbery, copyright © 1975 by John Ashbery, and is reprinted by permission of The Viking Press.

"Sentence" by Jerald Bullis is also from his book *Adorning the Buckhorn Helmet* to be published this year by Ithaca House, Ithaca, New York. Permission to reprint is by the author, Ithaca House, and *Western Humanities Review,* in which the poem originally appeared.

"At the Brooklyn Botanic Garden" by Alfred Corn, originally selected from *The New Yorker,* is also from the collection of poems, *All Roads at Once* by Alfred Corn, copyright © 1975 by Alfred Corn and reprinted by permission of The Viking Press.

"End of a Discourse on the Gentle (or Perhaps Slavish) Mentality" by D. J. Enright was selected from the printing in the January 1975 issue of *The Listener.* The poem is also from his collection *Sad Ires* published by Chatto and Windus Ltd., London.

Poetry Northwest has assigned the copyright to Norma Farber for her poem "A Lasting Supper."

"The Stone Child" by Elizabeth Harrod is to be included in an anthology *Explaining My Sex* to be published by Thorp Springs Press, Berkeley, California.

"The Last Covenant" by Naomi Lazard was selected from the first printing in the Spring 1975 issue of *The Massachusetts Review.* The poem is scheduled to be reprinted in *The Ardis Anthology of New American Poetry* published by Ardis Publishers, Ann Arbor, Michigan.

"A Refusal to Mourn" by Derek Mahon is also from Mr. Mahon's

CONTENTS

LOT: SOME SPECULATIONS

I mean what
did he do? one
minute there she

was, flesh of his
flesh, hustling
along beside

him, anxious
as ice cubes to
get away from

all that fire
and justice
on the plain,

and the next
she's a pillar
of wrath-

solid salt; it
was a hell
of a price,

even if her
curiosity was
morbid; what

did he do? you
could make a
case for not

even break-
ing stride, but
after all, it

was his wife; he
may have carved
a quick R.I.P.,

not looking
back, before
goosepimpling

on, or something
more sober-
ing, like BEWARE:

she may have
become a
kind of sodium-

chloride Ozymandias;
more likely she
wound up ground

up in some
market, or licked
to a nub

by beast-tongues,
yet there's
a chance, just

a chance, the
three of them
may have carted

her along, clear
to the cave,
where, in her corner,

cool as the moon,
she whitened
all that

wine and incest,
all that girled
conniving

for the
seed, the sons,
the tribes.

JON DRESSEL

A MOUNTAIN LION

her alarmed skulk
Fearing to peel her blending umber
From the background —
                                    her forefeet
Go forward daringly, a venture, a theft
                                    in them
Stealing her body away after —

She weaves, her banner's soft prisoner,
In her element of silence, weaving silence
Like a dance, a living silence
Making herself invisible magical steps
Weaving a silence into all her limbs

She flows along, just inside the air,
Every line eluding the eye. Hesitation
And moving beyond
And by hesitation. All her legs like
A magical multiplication of one leg —
Look at any one, the others are doing
                                    the walking.
And slender and pressing
Forward through silence, becoming silence
Ahead and leaving it behind, travelling
Like a sound-wave, arriving wary
                                    and sudden
Ahead of herself —
A swift stillness.

TED HUGHES

HOW IT IS

Shall I say how it is in your clothes?
A month after your death I wear your blue jacket.
The dog at the center of my life recognizes
you've come to visit, he's ecstatic.
In the left pocket, a hole.
In the right, a parking ticket
delivered up last August on Bay State Road.
In my heart, a scatter like milkweed,
a flinging from the pods of the soul.
My skin presses your old outline.
It is hot and dry inside.

I think of the last day of your life,
old friend, how I would rewind it, paste
it together in a different collage,
back from the death car idling in the garage,
back up the stairs, your praying hands unlaced,
reassembling the bites of bread and tuna fish
into a ceremony of sandwich,
running the home movie backward to a space
we could be easy in, a kitchen place
with vodka and ice, our words like living meat.

Dear friend, you have excited crowds
with your example. They swell
like wine bags, straining at your seams.
I will be years gathering up our words,
fishing out letters, snapshots, stains,
leaning my ribs against this durable cloth
to put on the dumb blue blazer of your death.

MAXINE KUMIN

CLANCY

We bought him at auction, tranquillized to a drooping halt,
A blue-roan burro to be ridden by infants in arms, by tyros
Or the feeblest ladies, to be slapped or curried or manhandled —
A burro for time exposures, an amiable lawnmower.

But he burst out of his delivery truck like a war-horse,
Figure-eighting all night at the end of his swivel chain,
Chin high, octuple-gaited, hee-hawing through two octaves
Across our field and orchard, over the road, over the river.

While I fenced-in our farm to keep him from barnstorming
Neighbors and dignified horses, then palisaded our house
Like a beleaguered fort, my wife with sugar and rolled oats
And mysteries of her own coaxed him slowly into her favor.

He stood through the muddiest weather, spurning all shelter,
Archenemy of gates and roofs, mangler of halters,
Detector of invisible hackamores, surefooted hoofer
Against the plots of strangers or dogs or the likes of me.

But she would brush him and whisper to him out of earshot
And feed him hazel branches and handfuls of blackberries
And run and prance beside him, while he goated and buck-jumped,
Then stood by the hour with his long soft chin on her shoulder

While I was left on the far side of my own fence
Under the apple trees, playing second pitchfork
Among a scattering of straw over the dark-gold burro-apples
Too powerful for any garden, even the Hesperides.

And I still watch from exile as, night or morning, they wander
Up slope and down without me, neither leading nor following
But simply taking their time over the important pasture,
Considering dew and cobwebs and alfalfa and each other.

And all his ancestors, once booted through mountain passes
Bearing their grubstaked packtrees, or flogged up dusty arroyos
To their bitter ends without water, are grazing now in the bottom
Of her mind and his, digesting this wild good fortune.

Dᴀᴠɪᴅ Wᴀɢᴏɴᴇʀ

WALKING OUT

Fishing alone in a frail boat,
he leaned too far, lost hold,
was turned out of the caulked world.
Seventy years he had lived without knowing
how surfaces keep the swimmer up.

In the green fall, the limbs' churn
of fear slowing to pavanne,
one breath held dear as a woman,
he searched for coins of light
in the pockets of terror,
counting oar-strokes backward:
shore was not far.

He did then what was given him to do.
As creatures of water once called on the future
locked in their bodies, he called on his past.
He walked, walked.
Time was enough, just enough, and luck.
Touching greenfingered sand, rising
and touching, the body bursting with useless
knowledge, he came to his height in air.

Back in his life now, he measures
distances one breath along, muses
wordless, flexing the oars of his legs.
    Things shimmer where he is:
    known woods and meadows,
    floors and streets raise walls around him
    the color of old glass.
    Heaven is a high, clear skin.

What he knows paces his green sleep.
All day the world wavers: wife,
sons, friends change.

Age has caught him, they say.
Beneath the drift of flesh his bones remember
trying for bottom.

He walks away.

BETTY ADCOCK

THE NAMES OF THE SURVIVORS

Trackers report signs of life, but as yet
no one knows the names of the survivors.
The passenger list has been released by the airline;
thirty-two persons were on board, including the crew
and one infant in arms; little else is known
at this hour about their identities.
They have come down in difficult terrain.
Rescue efforts are being made by men
trained in survival, backpacking in on foot —
pilots refuse to enter
this place of radio silence and demented winds,
canyons clawed in the rock by a vanished river,
country the Indians left to the talk of spirits,
saying whatever walks there leaves no tracks
and hunts the hunter; local sources tell us
that men who came out of this country alive
were given new names.

LINDA ALLARDT

ABSOLUTE CLEARANCE

Voilà, Messieurs, les spectacles que Dieu donne à
l'univers . . .
—Bossuet

He sees the pictures on the walls.
A sample of the truth only.
But one never has enough.
The truth doesn't satisfy.

In some vague hotel room
The linear blotches when dusk
Lifted them up were days and nights

And out over the ocean
The wish persisted to be a dream at home
Cloud or bird asleep in the trough
Of discursive waters.

The times when a slow horse along
A canal bank seems irrelevant and the truth:
The best in its best sample
Of time in relation to other time.

Suffer again the light to be displaced
To go down fuming
"So much is his courage high,
So vast his intelligence,
So glorious his destinies.

"Like an eagle that one sees always
Whether flying in the middle airs
Or alighting on some rock
Give piercing looks on all sides
To fall so surely on its prey
That one can avoid its nails
No less than its eyes."

How it would be clearer
Just to loaf, imagining little
(The fur of a cat in the sun):
Let the column of figures
Shift, add and subtract itself
(Sticks, numbers, letters)
And so on to median depth . . .

Until a room in some town
The result of a meeting therein
Clasping, unclasping
Toward the flustered look
Of toys one day put away for the last time.

"I put away childish things.
It was for this I came to Riverside
And lived here for three years
Now coming to a not uncertain
Ending or flowering as some would call it."

Teasing the blowing light
With its ultimate assurance
Severity of its curved smile
"Like the eagle
That hangs and hangs, then drops."

JOHN ASHBERY

SURVIVAL

The empty closet,
the missing suitcase,
the loveless house,
the fear that wanders
like a vapour,
closing throats,
squeezing small chests
in vises.
The wooden man
behind the locked door
too brittle for consolation,
too shattered to console.
We huddled, a small wolf-pack
planning survival.
Listing our own worth
in desperation.
The weeds would need
us in the sugarbeets,
the cattle bedded in
the far pasture wait
for barefoot boys at dawn.
At twelve I'm good with
orphan lambs, small calves,
chickens, and getting buttermilk
out of the spring.
The small brother rocked in
utter grief, moaning momma, momma,
till we slapped him into silence
being done with love and
other fairy tales.

G. Beadle

CONSIDERATIONS ON INDO-EUROPEAN CULTURE

the words for salmon
for birch tree
for willow
for wolf and bear

assure us that you were

women whom I remember
without any words at all

small and seldom-smiling
black hair braided

walking in the long grass
calling the wolves to your side

carrying on your hips
little clinging bear babies
little leaping salmon babies

giving them milk-weed pods
to suck on

cooking in the smokey hut
birch cloth wrapped around
tucked in
arms out-stretched unadorned

drinking honey beer with bread

lying down in the tawny dusk
salmon babies at the breast
bear babies at the breast

warm belly beds
for all the naked babies

nothing but skin between you
and all your skin the same skin
all smokey all downy all brown

all your words the same words
for birch and salmon and bear

JANET BEELER

REQUIEM

1

We will see no more
the mown grass fallen behind him
on the still ridges before night,
or hear him laughing in the crop rows,
or know the hard order of his delight.

Though the green fields are my delight,
elegy is my fate. I have come to be
survivor of many and of much
that I love, that I won't live to see
come again into this world.

Things that mattered to me once
don't matter any more.
I have left forever the safe shore
where any magnificence of art
could suffice my heart.

2

In the day of his work
when the grace of the world
was upon him, he made his way,
not turning back or looking aside,
light in his stride.

Now may the grace of death
be upon him, his spirit blessed
in deep song of the world
and the stars turning, the seasons
returning, and long rest.

WENDELL BERRY

STANDING STONE

The stone stands among new firs,
still overtopping them. Soon
they will hide it. Their lower branches
will find its cold bulk
blocking their growth. After years,
lopped trunks will lie piled
awaiting haulage. The stone will stand
in a cleared valley, and offer again
the ancient orientation.

The stone stores, transmits.
Against its almost-smoothness
I press my palms. I cannot ask,
having no word of power,
no question formed. Have I
anything to give? My hands offer
a dumb love, a hope towards
the day of the freed valley.
Flesh fits itself to the slow curve
of dominating stone, as prayer
takes the shape of a god's will.

A mindless ritual is not empty.
When the dark mind fails, faith lives
in the supplication of hands
on prayer-wheel, rosary, stone.
It is evening. I walk down-valley
on an old track. Behind me
the ephemeral trees darken.
Among them, the stone waits.

RUTH BIDGOOD

SCENARIO: THE EDIFICE

No doubt it is a prison. At its base
(we see depicted) here in coloured clays
stands the hill called Choukoutien, whose caves,
a litter of *coups de poing*, seeds, and crude quartz flakes,
are like the scooped-out skulls of men whose brains
were eaten. Outside is the grinding, groaning ice,
and at the door burns the Red Flower.
                                                    Abris
ring it, before which hides are strung from posts
to serve as windbreaks; also, piled stone walls.
   On its sides, earthworks, ringing a fortress
and labyrinth, threaded by a monster
horned like a bull. This is the bellowing cellar
   of a temple (as may be seen carved on this frieze)
from which go forth at noon grim-robed men
to strike off the heads of the tallest stalks of grain.
   Its upper reaches, though served by good roads
(the poet says) and aquaducts, are quite obscured
by clinging tenements, in which deposed
kings (here are statues of them, although much
defaced) and freed slaves starve, six to a room.
This part is blackened by fire,
                                         and topped
by many layers of chantries (shown in the tapestry)
humming with Glorias to the flatness of the Earth.
   Robed scholars (see the borders of the manuscript)
sit on their shoulders, each in his static cell
(the woodcut, which has been somewhat dubiously attributed
to a fifteen-year-old boy, shows that their belfries
were latterly much distracted by witches) attempting
to prove by logic the existence of God; but women
are forbidden to learn the language.

And there is
no doubt that the palace above this is glorious (see
the elevation by Uccello, the largest oil cartoon in the world);
though the tiles are slimy with blood, and the galleries
reek of gunpowder, they know there the world is round.
    But silence now, O Muse, for just above
A Shepherdess reclines, and dreams of Love.
Oblivious of th'Eternitie on which she stands,
Box'd like a Universe within her silken Bands,
The fair *Phyllida* rises from the Wrack,
And Locks of Hair distributes to the treacherous Pack
(Immortalised, it may be for a Week,
By some dumb Poet and his hunch-back'd Book).
    O larks! and now, from the sweet sleep of Earth, arise
on plumes of steam, and borne by slapping belts
(though these are not well shown in the daguerreotypes)
soot-smeared glassy palaces with plush-lined drawing rooms
haunted by pthisic ladies, foot by well-turned foot,
pure as the Innsbruck snow, and longing passionately
only to vote. They have good servants.
    The storey next, a noisy one, is much bedaubed
with mud and poppies, in which barbed wire's imbedded
(the photographs are all too clear for comfort; turn
the page) and fragile triple-wingéd beetles snarl about it.
    And at the very top (these X-ray plates are somewhat fogged)
intolerable mushroom-rose of light.
                    Yes, no doubt it is a prison,
but from here on up, one cannot see the walls;
they may be stars.
            (May we have the next slide, please?)
Ah. Embedded in this hand-axe is a tiny shell.
It is perhaps a hundred million years old.

                                    JAMES BLISH

SENTENCE

I have come to take an interest in
The redwing blackbird's quarrelling from
A spring swamp's tamarack stump —

How it adorns the wet air with a clarity
Iteration and the violent probabilities
That grow with the nights of the earth's

Turning might have something to do with —
I have come to take an interest in
Those versions of ongoingness that largely

Go on unseen: the cock woodcock's upward
Spiraling hosanna, that horny love song
Made of air and the windharps of his wings,

The stillness at the peak of want and song,
At the uttermost of his barrenness, that
Hovering at the nexus of his acres-wide based

Triangle woven in three dimensions at least
By the circles and ellipses of his rising lust;
Then the liquid twittering falling as from

Nowhere from that height, not straight
Down, but cutting through the prior arabesques
To land nearly where he started from —

Where dark lets the moon in to the aspen nubbins,
Where the horned owl gives the white pines half their dark,
Where the henbird waits like a clump of the wet, rich swamp.

JERALD BULLIS

VINCENT VAN GOGH

we are never the same
for his
madness.
for a single slash of wild yellow
yellows are never the same.
for the sanity of fire
for the sanity of sunflowers
for the sanity and insanity
we are changed
forever.

in the burning fields at Arles
mixing madness into oranges and reds
he challenged the sun.
he dared to create revelations.
no Icarus or Apollo he
flew beyond the blue boundaries of color
and fell,
a red-bearded eagle
screaming
at a white canvas.

he was to know
the antiseptic beds
of a stranger in his native land
and he became stranger still
a nighttime visitor to cypress trees
candles aflame in his sleepless hat,
he was to know,
we must believe this
that beyond the horizons of his canvas
was a world
where sanities and insanities
are simply colors
in fields of final yellow.

ISIDORE CENTURY

DEAD QUAIL

The sky cracked.
A piece fell. A flapping piece
with feathers and dark blood.
Wind parted when it fell;
grass opened, closed, and from it
rose a silence dark as blood.
I stood behind and watched the wind
move feathers back to life.
A leaf blew up, stuck against the moving blood,
I stood behind and waited for the ghost to give.
It wouldn't leave. It hovered like the bird it was.
Does this mean something, said the wind.
Does this mean nothing, said the grass.

The feathers lived against the losing blood.
The grass stood back, the sounding wind.
Send the ghost away, they said, the quail is dead.
They spoke together. Feather moved in blood
and still I watched, waiting for the ghost.

At last the blood was black and didn't move.
The feathers turned to sticks.
I was left behind
as wind divided for the ghost;
as grass first opened, silent,
and then, silent, closed.

ROSANNE COGGESHALL

AT THE BROOKLYN BOTANIC GARDEN

Another spring at the Garden, and how
Foolish to find myself heavy-hearted
On a day as sunny as this. Well,
The white cherries left me in a stupor,
As they always do. Let it go at that.

From a vender at the gate I've taken
A carton of childish, leather-tough
Popcorn, which winces saltily against
My teeth. Years since I've eaten any. . . .
Spring, like Christmas, is for children, maybe.

It belongs to the toddler just behind me,
Bobbing along under a pink balloon.
He's dribbling corn from a carton striped blue
Like mine. How much can he weigh, this tiny
Dollop of flesh? And how can the mere

Earth support one whose weight just suffices
To anchor a pink balloon? Heaviness,
Lightness, it's confused in my head, along
With blossoms, popcorn, the salts of childhood. . . .
I'm going to take a picture of that kid.

ALFRED CORN

THE HERO

for J.P.

Mother, when you suckled your child
did you know that you were suckling a hero?
Did you try & conceal him from the forces
of the dark? & now they found him out
& blew on the flame, the fire of virtue
burning too bright — for he was *ahead*
of his smile as the chariot's horses
were ahead of the victorious emperor
(thus the poet, his countryman). "Lasting"
would never tempt him; indifferent
to peril, he followed the only path
of his choice . . . Oh mother,
was he the same when in
the font they immersed him
as when in flames he ascended?

2

How else could they walk but in silence,
shuffling softly in Wenceslav Square,
hands drooping on their haunches,
eyes cast down & taste of ashes on tongue;
were not their feet objects of shame,
their feet that walked; their hands
that could grasp & hold!
Shame of the blood that flowed red (RED!)
in their veins while his young body was laid
in the earth blackened, inert, because the fire
of love had burnt brighter in him
than in us, brighter than life itself. . . .

MARGARET DIESENDORF

RINK KEEPER'S SESTINA: HOCKEY, HOCKEY

Call me Zamboni. Nights my job is hockey.
I make the ice and watch the kids take slapshots
At each other. They act like Esposito,
As tough in the slot as Phil, as wild with fury
In fights. Their coaches tell me this is pleasure.
But it isn't pleasure. What it is, is Hockey.

Now let me tell you what I mean by Hockey.
I mean the fights. I mean young kids in fury,
And all these coaches yelling for more slapshots.
I tell you, blood is spilled here. This is pleasure?
It seems to me the coaches should teach hockey,
Not how to act like Schultz or Esposito.

Look, I have nothing against Phil Esposito.
He's one of the greats, no question, it's a pleasure
To watch him play. My point is, why teach fury?
If I know life (at least if I know hockey),
Then fury's here to stay. We don't need Hockey
To tell us that, we don't need fights and slapshots.

Like yesterday. I heard a coach yell, "Slapshots!
Take slapshots, son! You think Phil Esposito
Hangs back? And hit! And hit again! That's hockey!"
But he was wrong. The kid was ten. That's Hockey.
You could tell the boy admired his coach's fury.
It won't be long before he hits with pleasure.

Sure, I'm no saint. I know. I've gotten pleasure
From fury, too, like any man. And hockey
At times gets changed around in me to Hockey.
I've yelled for blood at Boston Garden. Slapshots?
They've thrilled me. I've seen men clobber Esposito
And loved it when he hit them back with fury.

But you know what? Before these days of fury,
When indoor rinks were just a gleam in Hockey
Fanatics' eyes, there was no greater pleasure
Than winter mornings. Black ice. (Esposito
Knew days like this as a boy.) Some friends. No slapshots,
But a clear, cold sky. Choose teams. Drop the puck. Play hockey.

Yes, before big Hockey (sorry, Esposito),
Before the fury and all the blazing slapshots,
We had great pleasure outdoors playing hockey.

GEORGE DRAPER

HOMAGE TO GIACOMETTI

A

man

w
a
l
k
i
n
g

w
i
t
h
o
u
t

a

s
h
a
d
o
w

h
a
s

t
o

shine

STUART DYBEK

A WAY OUT

1

Time mocks but I would mock it,
Throw hurricane force against its devil,
Commanding it to stop. Flaunt a panorama
Of reality. Absolute. Here is the truth!
I want to look at the world as it is,
Look into the eye of a stopped eternity,
Believe in what I see, the great exemplars
Appearing on the stage of inner vision,
Elate, final, two radiant believers.

Here I see Buddha making the great denial,
Leaving his wife and child, having seen
A sick man, an old man, and a dead man,
Giving his life as a living sacrifice
To denial of appetite, dedicated to spirit.

And here I see that other master of mankind,
Jesus the subtle master of those who know,
Greater than Aristotle, to whom Plato
Had access, the daring revolutionist
Who knew that He would outlive Roman materialists.

These mocked the surly naturalism in man,
Said he was better, lit ways to lead him,
They covered the East and the West with light
And we in our faltering century have
To aid us blind Marx, Freud, blind Einstein;
Godlessness, fear, and relativity. Extinguish
These three their gross fanfares and bonfires,
While the serenity of Buddha and the fury of Christ
Give mankind examples of the way to go,
The ineffable, and the active means to know.

2

I walked on China, a young man, searching
The Buddha, I knew what he knew, but
A fierce Western passion drove me to Christ,
Exciting my membranes with His pure sacrifice.

The torment of His impossibility, the Nietzschean
Knowledge that there can be only one Christ,
Gave me the world-wrestle of two thousand years,
Doubt and belief warring in me to this day.

Also the impossibility of achieving Nirvana
Mismated me with the serene ideal of the East.
My warfare was that of rationality,
I could not abrogate my reason East or West.

Caught in this dilemma, I dreamed of time
And flung myself on the breast and body of nature.
Naturalism claimed me as day turned to night,
But I was struck twice by a binding light.

3

Now when ice comes over the river,
And boys skate before the coming of the snow,
How pleasant it is to sit by the Franklin stove,
Braced for ice and snow and thirty below.

And if we can endure the cold, and skis
Will take us turning down the trails,
And we can walk on snowshoes from the barn,
And drink the milk of goats new and warm,

We can live in nature as in our mother
Before we were born, and we can sense
That old death will give way to new life
As new mornings grow, Spring comes over the land.

RICHARD EBERHART

COAST OF MAINE

The flags are up again along the coast,
Gulls drop clams from a height onto the rocks,
The seas tend to be calm in July,
A swallow nests under our areaway,
It is high summer, the greatest days of the year,
Heat burgeoning the flowers, stones heating the tides,

This is peace, the indifference of nature, another year
Seeming the same as the year before,
The static ability of the world to endure.
There is Eagle Island twelve miles down the bay,
A mole has just dared to march over our garden,
The far islands seem changeless through decades.

Yet, think of the drama! Here am I,
One year older into inevitability,
The country torn in honor's toss-out,
What does nature care about the nature of man?
Three hundred years ago along this coast
The Europeans came to confront the Indians,

Yet the Ice Age shaped these shores millions
Of years ago, unimaginable upon our senses,
What do I say to the beneficent sun
Descending over the pine trees, the sun of our planet?
What does it care for the nature of man,
Its virile essence unassimilable?

Here come the hummingbirds, messengers
Of fragility, instantaneous as imagination,
How could they be so iridescent-evanescent,
Quick-darters, lovers of color, drinkers of nectar?
Do they remind us of a more spirited world
When everything was lithe, and quick, and visionary?

RICHARD EBERHART

END OF A DISCOURSE ON THE GENTLE (OR PERHAPS SLAVISH) MENTALITY

And when you go to the wall
(As you will)
You'll find that even the high one
Around the graveyard
Is no protection.
You lie in the way of a natural by-pass,
As illicit as a sick hedgehog.

And when you get to heaven
(As you will)
Then you'll be told
That you are more to blame than they,
If you hadn't been the way you were
They wouldn't have acted the way they did.

'The Fathers of a city
Lesser though not unlike the present
Ruled that slaves were fit for freedom
Only if enslavement so disgusted them
They took their lives.
We have a rule excluding suicides.'

And as you wait there, puzzling it out
(A kind of talk you've heard before
Shuffling your feet as you listened,
Conscious of the justice of it,
Paying mute tribute to the rest of it)
They'll push past you at the gate.

'The disposal of this class of souls
Presents as much embarrassment
As does the laying of their bones.'

Its own reward,
It will have to be its own reward.

D. J. ENRIGHT

A LASTING SUPPER

A half century later,
I'm finally coming into the taste
of separation. Really. That light piquant spread
of distance we used to lay between us,
was mere hunger-ration. This is a feast
threatening never to end. Must I still eat?

Must I, filled, still eat
while the heavy banquet lasts later
with every tolling month? To feast
without relief is to lose the taste
for food. Let there be small famines between us.
Let such infinities as spread

into malady, shrivel. Widespread,
this table gluts me faint, for I eat
the years. And still the board groans between us,
heaping our division. Later, later!
my tongue implores. Impossible to taste
an undiminishing absence. . . . But the feast

insists. Famished for want of you, I must feast
on want. Survival is my spread
surfeit: grossly deadening, foretaste
of death. O let me starve on live crumbs. To overeat
is morbidly to suffocate hunger. Later
I'll need that hunger — should there arise between us

some bare subsistence: some nothing between us,
an essence, in a place where feast
is a kind of fast. Later,
I think, eternity may spread
so spare refreshment, we can eat
innocently again. Together we'll taste

the frugal air among our atoms: day-taste
and night-taste pure vintages between us.
Meal of simple starlight we can sheerly eat.

Norma Farber

FOR I PRAISE YOU, CHRISTOPHER SMART

For you saw divinity in your cat's electrical skin

For you wrote electrical poems

For you wrote cows & shops & trees & earlobes shaking
with the charge of God

For you fell down sputtering prayers in the street

For you fell down sputtering prayers just about everywhere

For they called you crazy, which is one way of putting it,
& they locked you up

For you generated celebrations even in the madhouse

For you observed the madhouse like the painter before
the gingko trees, looking again & again to catch the color
under the color

For you heard atoms snapping in root hairs & the halo humming
round the whole electrical scene

For I praise you, Christopher Smart, for losing your wits
in the Age of Reason

SUSAN FAWCETT

A MAN AND A WOMAN

Between a man and a woman
The anger is greater, for each man would like to sleep
In the arms of each woman who would like to sleep
In the arms of each man, if she trusted him not to be
Schizophrenic, if he trusted her not to be
A hypochondriac, if she trusted him not to leave her
Too soon, if he trusted her not to hold him
Too long, and often women stare at the word men
As it lives in the word women, as if each woman
Carries a man inside her and a woe, and has
Crying fits that last for days, not like the crying
Of a man, which lasts a few seconds, and rips the throat
Like a claw — but because the pain differs
Much as the shape of the body, the woman takes
The suffering of the man for selfishness, the man
The woman's pain for helplessness, the woman's lack of it
For hardness, the man's tenderness for deception,
The woman's lack of acceptance, an act of contempt
Which is really fear, the man's fear for fickleness,
Yet cars come off the bridge in rivers of light
Each holding a man and a woman.

ALAN FELDMAN

ROOM 635, WING B

Father lay in the crib.
His eyes struggled like moths to reach the light.
His nose tunneled the dark.

The curse of life lay on the children.
The curse of life lay on the wife.
They stood around the bed.

"Nurse, Nurse, get the Nurse . . ."

Liquid trickles from the mast;
a blood bag hangs at the feet.

"He was big enough to spank a little girl," his daughter says.
"He was big enough to eat up little boys," his sons report.
"His nice-nice was the world to me," stated his wife.

Who put this dummy here, in place
of Father dear?

Room 635, Wing B.
The sky is a silent film.
The window a dead end; heat hisses
like a gas
pulling us into sleep . . .

Quick, quick
fetch the basin, Father's sick.

"He's so big
when he fell
one arm knocked a building down.
The Rockies were his pocket comb."

From the clouds, reproachful:
"Oh where were you? Why weren't you
here?"

"There, there,
there, there."

Uncovered, thin yellow legs.
Don't look,
Canaan was cursed.

Shh, outside the legend grows:
how prodigious the energy,
crayoned yellow sun with spiky crown.
Shh . . .

But what are we to do with this body?
The air leaking from it
is filling us up.

The pressure is intolerable;
we are ballooning
into grownups,
set to drift.

Two black queens
trundle you away—

rag doll, Thunderer,
leaf.

CELIA GILBERT

THE AWAKENING

You could see thick fibres of
muscle break into the light
     as he swung to turn his back
to the girl: she could still see
the dying flash of his face
       immense in front of her eyes. He was

the stranger who had touched her
and turned her with his fingers
     until she was a flower beneath his
touch. Her caught limbs quivered in delicate breath

as he brought her to the edge of a darkness
where all things begin: Adam
and Eve whirling through space in rocketships
cluttered with beasts chattering to no end the undying secret
      of their unbroken lust. Something wobbled and

suddenly jerked. The moon was barren, full of
rocks. Her hair, undone
     of her sleep, would have to be combed
for work, twenty strokes of the brush. It was
just a thought. In the dark
     of the morning she walks
to where the world is, for a second time, to begin

GREGORY GRACE

SOME POSSIBILITIES

There you were, standing in an empty field,
cold as ever, kicking a stone to see if it moved.
Minding your own business.

And there he was, perfect stranger,
breaking up the light, moving
as if he knew where he was going.

He was perfect, two arms, two legs,
and making the most of them,
coming toward you as if
there were no such thing as distance.

He must mistake you for someone else.
You are the sparrow biting its tongue,
the rock left in the middle of the field,
too large to be moved.

He is inventing you as he goes.
He is picking a bouquet of wild flowers.
You think he could pass through you

and never notice.
He thinks he could surround you.
"What else are these arms for?" he would say.

As if by the time he arrives, you will be there.

DEBORA GREGER

IN THE MUSEUM GARDEN

Always dying into ourselves,
coming back into sunlight . . .
Your face beside me is a frieze
of shadows, many things
wake there and go to sleep.

This day we walked through the galleries,
steeped in the glory of echoes.
A bitter dragon smoked on his pedestal,
the stone horses stamped
in their marble fields,
under glass the jade belly
of a goddess seemed to me to tremble.

We halted before a mountain
towering in silk,
climbed a pathway footworn
by the steep passion of the anchorite
to a bench of hand-quarried stone,
and sat there dreaming
in a shower of blackbirds.

There is so much flowering around us,
so much color burning the plum bough;
summer dense and smoldering
in the teahouse throng, the gold carp
of the emperor floating in green water;
your body, loved and ageless
in its printed sunlight.

And much that is dying . . .
In the faces blurring to leaflight
as we walk, the words of water
spoken from the trees; the city traffic
a towering noise beyond the gate—
a speech already strange.
And now in the shadow that deepens
in the fabled archway.

We lean on the boredom of princes
who built their palace of air
and leaves, and sank in the stale
histories of these halls and ledgers.

They left us wandering in a peopled
grove, listening at nightfall
to the grave echoes in stone:
our voices steeped in this closing hour,
our own footsteps leaving the garden.

JOHN HAINES

THE STONE CHILD

I carried you in my belly
inert as a stone
on the floor of a cave
The fifth month I miscarried you
When you were born you had been dead two months.

I cannot remember your exit
only the blood soaking the towels
one clot smooth as a piece of liver
and the great knot of roots that nourished you.

Did you, when the doctor
pressed on my belly
slip out a little stone fish
smash like a clenched fist
or fall into his hands
a carved white quartz
image of a child.

I took back your brother
took him into me, into the cave
my uterus a mouth eating him
as the earth eats you.

I do not know where you are.
What did the doctor do with you
did he flush you away
or carry you away in his black bag
Do you sleep now, stone child
my quartz son
in some glass uterus
waiting to be born?

I carry you in my mind like a stone.

ELIZABETH HARROD

MAKING THINGS GROW

All day we've had to haul around
and readjust the garden hose's coils
to keep the mouths in that thin soil
kissed evenly. They must be loose,
unpuckered. I want them ready
to receive the sun, and wildly,
the way our daughter wrings milk out
when she makes her bottle chirp
or drinks up sleep, her paws curled
as if clutching out at it; the way
she digests the yawn that widens
through her arms each time she hoists
herself upright with her hands, or laps
up what it is she studies in my eyes.
That's what the garden, though it won't
wake me up at night, expects of me;
what all unkissed places everywhere
expect, the tongue expects, what this
lonely place on the neck expects and
what, on tiptoe, this place on the
throat expects and what this
neglected place expects, what this
place here expects. And this place
here. And here.

JONATHAN HOLDEN

SIX POEMS FROM THE SEQUENCE: LUMB'S REMAINS

1

In the M5 Restaurant
Our sad coats assemble at the counter

The tyre face pasty
The neon of plaster flesh
With little inexplicable eyes
Holding a dish with two buns

Symbolic food
Eaten by symbolic faces
Symbolic eating movements

The road drumming in the wall, drumming in the head

The road going nowhere and everywhere

My freedom
Is to feed my life
Into a carburettor

Petroleum has burned away all
But a still-throbbing column
Of carbon-monoxide and lead.

I attempt a firmer embodiment
With illusory coffee
And a gluey quasi-pie.

2
Before-dawn twilight, a sky dry as tale

The horizons
Bubbling with bird voices

The blackbird arrives a yard away, in a black terror
And explodes off
As if searching for a way out
Of a world it has just been flung into.

The shrews, that have never seen man, are whizzing everywhere.

Who is that tall lady walking on our lawn?

The star in the sky is safe.

The owl on the telegraph pole
Warm and dry and twice his right size
Scratches his ear.

Under the stones are the woodlice, your friends.

3
Let that one shrink into place
Camouflaged and doggo
Under his eye-wall
Like an overlooked lizard.

Let the madman thrash in his pram
And the fool harden his opinion
And the man of bile
Deify his will,

And that one, the eagle-nosed, the broad-handed
Be above the battle — i.e. lie
Carcase under it, cheek turned
To the propitiation of the blow-fly.

Let you keep one world nearer the world
Simple as those puffball rabbits
Who multiply themselves, in abandon and joy

For what seem to be foxes.

4

Stilled at his drink

Old, in his body's deadfall.
His body fills the whole stage.

Spirit has all evaporated
Coolly as alcohol

From the bulbous blue weldings
Of his knuckles, from his whiskery eye-sockets.
Illusion
Cannot raise the energy.

General closure
Has confessed him.

Throat of primordial Iguana
Brain of dried herbs.

He sits — idol of some extinct religion.
The dust worships his feet.

He stares
Into — some wateriness.

Jilted
For the last time.

5

The bulging oak is not as old
As the crooked tree of blood
In the body of the girl
Who marvels at it.

The tree, too, knows its owner.

When she walked away the history oak
That leaned over immortal water
Fell in a flurry of shadows
Ghosting away downstream.

6

Why do you take such nervy shape to become
A victim, so violin-like?

The Inquisitors have caught you.
Now you are under the discretion

Of their fingers and smiles.
'Where do you come from?'

You cannot speak their tongue.
You can only cry wordlessly

Crying sideways
From the eyes of men, to the shut doors

Of the dust-grains. Shaking the dust

Of the wrong world.

TED HUGHES

WAITING FOR THE FIRST CHILD

Outside the window October crackles
And burns   the old orchard opens
And the sun falls further away

Cornfields and maples stand empty
As abandoned houses   all month long
I had felt the chilly fullness

Of water turning darkly over
It is what my skin forgets
At night in blankets in dreams

Of green picnics of the whiteness
Of eggs of a warm place
By the rock where we sat

And you the slimmest of women
Stretching into your final roundness
And everything red even the canoe

Arcs like the evening hills
Beneath the three hemlocks
And while we are there before dark

You say you hurt with rhythms
Of the season of everything
Sinking to its own level

But in the deep leaves
As we listen to the pheasants crowing
We say

Child
It is the end of October
And you are late in your promise

But we will wait for you all night long
By the full moon with the owl's wings
Rising like the beginning of pain

Around us in the contracting dark.

HARRY HUMES

IT IS THE SEASON

when we learn
or do not learn
to say goodbye.

The crone leaves that as green
virgins opened themselves
to sun, creak at our feet

and all farewells return
to crowd the air:
say, Chinese lovers by a bridge,

with crows, and a waterfall;
he will cross
the bridge, the crows fly;

children, who told each other
secrets and will not speak
next summer.

Some speech of parting
mentions God, as in
a Dieu, Adios,

commending what cannot
be   kept
to permanence.

There is nothing of north
unknown, as the dark
comes earlier. The birds

take their lives in their wings
for the cruel trip.
All farewells are rehearsals.

Darling, the sun rose
later, today.
Summer, summer

is what we had.
Say nothing yet.
Prepare.

JOSEPHINE JACOBSEN

BURNING THE BODY'S FENCES

Stepping through my flesh, leaving it
Over my shoulder
Like a burnt doorframe,

I follow again the bitch hound
To a child's grave
Where stars kneel at the speed
Of light
And the mushroom stands unsexed.

I know there is a darkness so sinewy
Its silence
Clabbers the milk still hidden away
In the grassblades

And forces the dawn
Back down the rooster's throat.

I have heard my body
Reamed out, auricle and vein
By something
That rejoices on the heart's slopes
Like a knife
Traveling on the glint of its own blade.

At noon, disguised as a dragonfly,
I admired
The cool cheeks of the headstones

And the chiselled out initials
That just missed
Spelling my name.

THOMAS JOHNSON

HOLE IN THE CHOIR

There is a hole in the choir.
A burnt-out space
Among the faces
As though a penny hummed
Hot with overload
In the fusebox.

A hole like that chewed
Into a sleeve, the elbow
Rawed from shoring up
Boredom's mulish head.

It is the navel
Of the hymn to the glories
Of God, teaching us
All praise
Comes from the belly.

Notch by notch grown
Unchurchly, I tighten my belt
And by buckle-glint, learn

To move again
In the wail-papered rooms
Of my father's whippings,

See among the welts
He raised on my leg

That one red road
Down which I've come
To love him,

To love the hole in the choir,
That soloist
Who will neither sing
Nor be seated.

THOMAS JOHNSON

WAIT

Wait, for now.
Distrust everything, if you have to.
But trust the hours. Haven't they
carried you everywhere, up to now?
Personal events will become interesting again.
Hair will become interesting.
Pain will become interesting.
Buds that open out of season will become interesting.
Secondhand gloves will become lovely again;
their memories are what give them
the need for other hands. And the desolation
of lovers is the same; that enormous emptiness
carved out of such tiny beings as we are
asks to be filled;
the need for the new love *is* faithfulness to the old.

Wait.
Don't go too early.
You're tired. But everyone's tired.
But no one is tired enough.

Only wait a little, and listen—
music of hair,
music of pain,
music of looms weaving all our loves again.

Be there to hear it, it will be the only time,
most of all to hear
the flute of your whole existence,
rehearsed by the sorrows, play itself into total exhaustion.

GALWAY KINNELL

HANDS

If the tongues would still themselves
the hands could talk, who knows but that
they know the earth as well, can dance
in air better than words. Who knows,
they are never still. Who knows but
we assign them the wrong things,
places of would be permanence, improvements
of saw and nail, garbage to carry out.
For all this yet I knew once hands so
delicate, so sure on me, they brought me
song. And for that dignity again I would
be still.

GREG KUZMA

THE LAST COVENANT

for the wolves

The sun marks the sea with a sign,
last bright sickle of light.
We drive the wind before us
into the darkness, quickly
across the domain of waters, fast

as your fur and my hair can fly.
What a bird would say I feel
on my lips; the words breaking out
in pairs, two by two as those other
animals went from the flood.

Moonlight flickers and melts
on the air; one final leap
into the deep night and we hit
land. Now we're creeping like sap
from a tree while the ground is wet

underfoot, and the beetle's sound
is a gong. On our knees in the end,
back to the roots of the heart.
This is the place, the wind
made flesh; the greens and all

movement are one. We can just see
the brilliant faces of cubs
looking out. All night I must kneel
at the gates of the house without
doors. Morning comes like a knife

between my eyes. I must roll back
my tongue and forget my own
language of lies. Then my body
remembers, my feet grow as sure
as your own of these deepest

retreats where we all sleep
together. The ways of the trees
open for me, defying with love
the guns, the numbers of enemies
who are stalking the woods

where we live now as we should live,
our bodies close as the ringing
of bells. I am one with you at last,
a guardian of paradise,
with a helmet of fiery leaves

and nothing more. I know we will not
survive. I see us already ablaze,
trapped in a circling fire.
The killers stand on its edge,
triggers cocked, quick on the draw

and ready. We have only this
moment. You push your face
into my hand; I hold you hard
at my side, bless you again.
A cry holds us both in its arms.

NAOMI LAZARD

HOPKINS IN DUBLIN

The terror of this triple night turns
All England dark within me. All England
Source and sink of soaring where once
Birds thrilled me; then flight turned dirtward:
A grappling with wings, with anxious hands
That grip the chalice now in holy dread.
Dark soul, dark town, dark night
Scheme within this brain where words
Tumble, fumble for the light of Saxon
Down and fell, for the light
That blazed in Essex, Oxford, and when I touched
Duns Scotus in the North, in Scotland, in Wales,
When England and myself were one,
Hawk and sky, plough and earth, and I sang
No songs to please these somber Gaels.

Plain now, in this Irish night, delight
I had once in subtle glows: a farmer's phrase,
A counterpoint, the proper solid words
For trout or fall. The Subtle One spoke,
I listened and seven years were seven days
When I knew silence had an end.
Heart swung shapes for sounds, brain pitched
Cow and grass and grove to songs I would hurrah
For human ears: nun or weeping child
Or Bishop, whose ring I longed to kiss.

Who knows when scruple first said *Saint?*
When first I mistook fame scorned
For holiness, made fame and beauty one?
I thought, I wrote, I pled, I fell
Into a darkness where my soul was torn
By poem and prayer. My soul,
Source and sink of all my singing now,
Became a ghost I sought and shrank from:
Dark soul, darker than these dark souls
That fill these dark churches wringing

Their imagined sins before a Lord
Stern as stone, grey as these awful homes
They've built—a Lord just in more ways
Than I dreamed when spring stirred in me
Stark skies, shot through with drifting bones.

Here night rides the ancient sea like Danes
Into the land, striding bodies down with sleet
And wind. I ache, I freeze, I sweat,
I offer naked flesh to naked bed,
I reckon death and find it sweet,
Sweeter than that fame I scorned.
Ah, fame the fisher still reels, still hooks
My soul, now tugs me toward the wreck
Of flesh, toward the final irony:
A poet making God, not books,
The tool of fame. No, not poet, priest
With simple words for simple men—

Irish men tormented by an awful lack
Of carnelian leaf, of beryl lake—
My words again, my sins.

I have hedged on every sacrifice and now,
Hedged in by lies, I must unlie the past.
Robert has my poems; those who read them
Will make of them their own feeble failures:
Kilns where human underthought will cast
Busts of justice, substitutes for faith.
Remember, at the end I tried to write
A wedding song and sonnets of despair,
Tried to mix Duns Scotus and Saint Patrick
And make wine, not wormwood, of this triple night.

What I have made I drink.
Taste, sound, color, spinning hawk and rod,
Thick-faced farmers, quick wind and swelling cloud,
Speckled wings, springs, seas and dingles rolling
Sing God, shout God but (my God!) are not God.

WARREN LEAMON

RASPBERRIES

Once, as a child, I ate raspberries. And forgot.
And then, years later,
A raspberry flowered on my palate, and the past
Burst in unfolding layers within me.
It tasted of grass and honey.
You were there, watching and smiling.
Our love unfolded in the taste of raspberries.

More years have passed; and you are far, and ill;
And I, unable to reach you, eating raspberries.
Their dark damp red, their cool and fragile fur
On the always edge of decay, on the edge of bitter,
Bring a hush of taste to the mouth

Tasting of earth and of crushed leaves
Tasting of summer's insecurity,
Tasting of crimson, dark with the smell of honey

Tasting of childhood and of remembered childhood,
And now, now first, the darker taste of dread.

Sap and imprisoned sunlight and crushed grass
Lie on my tongue like a shadow,
Burst like impending news on my aching palate

Tasting not only of death (I could bear that)
But of death and of you together,
The folded layers of love and the sudden future,
Tasting of earth and the thought of you as earth

As I go on eating, waiting for the news.

LAURENCE LERNER

THE MOON MOMENTS

The faint starlight rolls restlessly on the mat.
Those women talking outside have clouds passing across
their eyes.
Always there is a moon that is taking me somewhere.
Why does one room invariably lead into other rooms?

We, opening in time our vague doors,
convinced that our minds lead to something never allowed
before,
sit down hurt under the trees, feeding it simply because
it is there, as the wind does, blowing against the tree.

Yet time is not clairvoyant,
and if it has the answer to our lives, proud
in its possession of that potential which can change
our natures,
beating the visions of childhood out of us,

the socialism and the love,
until we remain awkwardly swung to the great north of
honour.
What humility is that which will not let me reveal the
real?
What shameful secret lies hidden in the shadows of my
moon?

All these years; our demands no longer hurt our eyes.
How can I stop the life I lead within myself?
The startled, pleading question in my hands lying in my
lap
while the gods go by, triumphant, in the sacked city
at midnight?

JAYANTA MAHAPATRA

A REFUSAL TO MOURN

for Maurice Leitch

He lived in a small farmhouse
At the edge of a new estate.
The trim gardens crept
To his door, and car engines
Woke him before dawn
On dark winter mornings.

All day there was silence
In the bright house. The clock
Ticked on the kitchen shelf,
Cinders moved in the grate,
And a warm briar gurgled
When the old man talked to himself;

But the doorbell seldom rang
After the milkman went,
And if a coat-hanger
Knocked in an open wardrobe
That was a great event
To be pondered on for hours

While the wind thrashed about
In the back garden, raking
The roof of the hen-house,
And swept clouds and gulls
Eastwards over the lough
With its flap of tiny sails.

Once a week he would visit
An old shipyard crony,
Inching down to the road
And the blue country bus
To sit and watch sun-dappled
Branches whacking the windows

While the long evening shed
Weak light in his empty house,
On the photographs of his dead
Wife and their six children
And the Missions to Seamen angel
In flight above the bed.

'I'm not long for this world'
Said he on our last evening,
'I'll not last the winter,'
And grinned, straining to hear
Whatever reply I made;
And died the following year.

In time the astringent rain
Of those parts will clean
The words from his gravestone
In the crowded cemetery
That overlooks the sea
And his name be mud once again

And his boilers lie like tombs
In the mud of the sea bed
Till the next ice age comes
And the earth he inherited
Is gone like Neanderthal Man
And no records remain.

But the secret bred in the bone
On the dawn strand survives
In other times and lives,
Persisting for the unborn
Like a claw-print in concrete
After the bird has flown.

DEREK MAHON

THE ANGEL OF DEATH IS ALWAYS WITH ME

The Angel of Death is always with me—
the hard wild flowers of his teeth,
his body like cigar smoke
swaying through a small town jail.

He is the wind that scrapes through our months,
the train wheels grinding over our syllables.
He is the footstep continually pacing through our chests,
the small wound in the soul,
the meteor puncturing the atmosphere.
And sometimes he is merely a quiet between the start of an act
and its completion,
a silence so loud
it shakes you like a tree.

It is only then you look up from the wars,
from the kisses,
from the signing of the business agreements.
It is only then you observe the dimensions
housed in the air of each day,
each moment;
only then you hear the old caressing the cold rims of their sleep,
hear the middle-aged women in love with their pillows
weeping into the gray expanse of each dawn,
where young men, dozing in alleys,
envision their loneliness to be a beautiful girl
and do not know they are part of a young girl's dream,
as she does not know that she is a dream in the sleep
of middle-aged women and old men,
and that all are contained in a gray wind
that scrapes through our months.

But soon we forget that the dead sleep in buried cities,
that our hearts contain them in ripe vaults.
We forget that beautiful women dry into parchment
and ball players collapse into ash;
that geography wrinkles and smoothes like the expressions on a face,
and that not even children
can pick the white fruit from the night sky.

And how *could* we laugh while looking at the face
that falls apart like wet tobacco?
How could we wake each morning
to hear the muffled gong beating inside us,
our mouths full of shadows, our rooms filled with a black dust?

Still,
it is humiliating to be born a bottle:
to be filled with air, emptied, filled again;
to be filled with water, emptied, filled again;
and, finally, to be filled with earth.

And yet I am glad that The Angel of Death is always with me:
his footsteps quicken my own,
his silence makes me speak,
his wind freshens the weather of my day.
And it is because of him
I no longer think
that with each beat
my heart
is a planet drowning from within
but an ocean filling for the first time.

MORTON MARCUS

THE BITTERN

Because I have turned my head for years
in order to see the bittern
I won't mind not finding
what I am looking for
as long as I know it could be there,
the cover is right,
it would be natural.

I loved you for what you had seen
and because you took me to see things,

alpine flowers
and your heart under your shirt.

The birds that mate for life
we supposed to be happiest,

my green-eyed
bitter evergreen . . .

The bough flies back into the night.

I might be driving by a marsh
and suddenly turn my head —
That's not exactly the way you see them you say.
So I look from the corners of my eyes
as if cheating in school
or overcoming a shyness.

In the end I see
                    nothing
but how I go blindly on loving
a life from which something is missing.

Clouds rushing across the sun,
gold blowing down on the reeds —

nothings like these . . .

SANDRA McPHERSON

THE DOG IS 12

Squiggly, O, puddler, gob of spunk
Bonnet blue goodness
You have found some meat
They, at the table, tease you with a dummy
You glom it greedily,
still squeeze the meat like mud
through your kuckles
Classy punk, throatless gargler
a laugh in a fist

Jellybelly muffin, you take your prize,
crawl over to the dog
asleep under a chair
in his gray foot-to-knee world
You search for something in the dog's skin,
knead,
pull folds of shoulder and neck skin back
Fleas scatter themselves

Your father is dredging your deserted pablum
planets stir,
and calling. You flange your attention
The old dog grins
lifts that patted-flat head
and sniffs your hand
Grinny pumpkin, O, hit man
you club the old head
The dog plays, convincingly, dead.

CRAIG MILLAGE

CECROPIA TERZINE

I found one fall snugged tight onto its twig
A tapered swelling spun, a woven chamber
Milkweed-pod shapely, roughly half that big,

And like a pod which has by late September
Split open, split its cottonseeds and dried
To wrapping-paper lightness. Was this slumber?

A death? The chamber seemed unoccupied
And much unraveled at the tip, though shaken
It rattled as if *something* were inside—

A walnut in its hull . . . I'd touched the broken
Skyblue or speckled cups of songbird eggs
And shells of locusts, each a hollow icon

Still clinging to the bark with empty legs,
And loved their one-time tenants' winged completion;
And, knowing well what fragile sorts of dregs

Cicadas, sparrows, seeds leave, my impression
Of this cocoon's light dryness kept me quite
From seeing any signs of occupation.

And that was why, one January night,
I jerked awake for such a ghostly reason:
Somewhere I'd heard the thumping-flopping flight

Of wings shut up in darkness and in prison,
Doggedly feckless. Hangers crashed and clanged
Another terrifying diapason.

I lay a long time while the trapped wings banged
Themselves on wood and wire in their trouble
And blindly ricocheted and boomeranged

And flop-thumped till exhaustion wore them feeble
Inside the only closet in my room.
And when I switched a lamp on and felt able

To open it
              there toppled from the gloom
Heavily sideways, stunned by light, a glory
Huge as a plate, with tiny, perfect, plume-

Like new antennae, feet red-orange and furry,
Thick furry abdomen, each panting wing
Powdered with cocoa-colored plush and starry

With one rich eyespot. Months before the spring
My lamplit nights had brought him forth in splendor,
Mad with an urge that powered his battering:

Break free and find your mate O find her find her!
My windowsills lay inches deep in snow
The females meant for him were sleeping under.

Born out of season, twenty years ago.
The wasteful barren death of so much beauty
Must hurt me till my own. I've come to know

Too well since that cold night in Cincinnati
What barren is, and for my sorry crime
Begun to know a terror and a pity

Unsayable save through this keeping time,
These saving graces slanted rhyme and rhyme.

JUDITH MOFFETT

L'EMPIRE DES LUMIÈRES

It is the house that we shall come to
after a summer day's long progress
through woods and clearings, through ourselves,
charting those areas too green
and too heat-burdened not to matter.

It is dusk when we come upon it,
the sky pale blue, crowding the poplars
rumor of fragrance, stir of darkness,
coolness welling beneath the surface,
denoting, somewhere, fall of evening,

each leaf in silhouette so clear,
so painfully acute the focus,
we shall remember it as landscape,
landscape, or dreamscape, or projection,
glimpsed, if not dreamt, as though through fever.

Within the house one light is burning,
lamplight streaming from those two windows
on the second floor, to the left,
which we will know is our room since
no other lamps have yet been lit.

Outside, a streetlight etches shadows
over the stucco's white facade,
tenderly slips refraction's bracelets
on the arm of the little lake
on which the villa has been set.

There will be a table, a bed,
a sheet so white taut on the mattress
we sense we travel in a province
where girls still gather at the river
to beat the laundry with flat stones.

clarity after clarity
having had light fall from our shoulders,
having had thirst assail our lips,
what we will say, or drink, or eat,
beyond all meat and wine before this,

darker than crusts on which we nourished
fiercer than words we hoped to speak,
what luster we will seek out, live with,
what blindness apprehend as sight,
there seems no way of naming yet.

When the light goes out, as it must,
when the stars, in that demonstration
of unparalleled depth and order,
let down their lines to graze the water
and the wind makes the lake pure silk,

clarity after clarity
will have been visited on our eyes,
will have blinded us in our lives,
made the champagne taste more like water
than we would have thought possible.

Darkness will deepen, as will we,
tenderness after tenderness
break our lips, burden our hands,
complicate passion, fashion context,
past simplification simplify.

Tomorrow there are expeditions
into the fields of light itself
of such promise, such penetration,
of so pronounced a dedication,
that we will hardly sleep tonight.

Who we will be with one another,
what we will suffer, say, become,
the ends of risk, commitment, travel,
will loom as intimate, as lucid,
as fever we have seen through clearly.

HERBERT MORRIS

SHORELINES

Someday I'll wake and hardly think of you;
You'll be some abstract deity, a myth—
Say Daphne, if you knew her as a tree.
Don't think I won't be grateful. I will be.
We'd shuck the oysters, cool them off with lime,
Spice them with Tabasco, and then scoop them up,
Who thought we were in Paradise. We were not.
Three couples and three singles shared that house
For two weeks in September. Wellfleet stayed
Remarkable that fall. And so did we.
Confessions, confidences kept us up
Half the night; the dawn birds found us still
Dead tired, clenched on the emotional,
Which led to two divorces later on,
Recriminations, torn-up loyalties,
The dreariness of things gone wrong for good.
Yet who could forget those wet, bucolic rides,
Drunk dances on the beach, the bonfires,
The sandy lobsters not quite fit to eat?
Well, there were other falls to come as bad,
But I still see us on a screened-in porch,
Dumbly determined to discover when
The tide turned and the bay sank back in mud.
We'd watch it carefully, hour after hour,
But somehow never could decide just when
The miracle occurred. Someone would run
Into the marshes yelling, "Where's the shore?"
We hardly see each other anymore.

HOWARD MOSS

THE METAL WAR

He came home from the war. It was so big
it needed no capital letters, and he
was still shorter than his wife by an inch.
He had no medals, but a glittering tapeworm
in his belly shared his mother's raisin pie
and hearty toasts of brandy from his pa.
In the night, his love's soft hand
went gliding on his back, where silver shreds
of shrapnel ground their tiny decorations
in his spine. One golden morning he awoke
and found one side of his face had stiffened.
He blinked one eye and wrinkled half his forehead,
smiled crookedly and went off to the doctor
who told him to relax and rest. That night
he felt just half her kiss and had to close one eye
with his finger. In his dreams the faces flattened
into large glistening coins. She finally learned
to draw her fingers back from the abyss.

JOYCE NELSON

THE BACKWARD LOOK

As once in heaven Dante looked back down
From happiness and highest certainty
To see afar the little threshing floor
That makes us be so fierce, so we look now
And with what difference from this stony place,
Our sterile satellite with nothing to do,
Not even water in the so-called seas.

No matter the miracles that brought us here,
Consider the end. Even the immense power
Of being bored we brought with us from home
As we brought all things else, even the golf
Balls and the air. What are we doing here,
Foreshadowing the first motels in space?
"They found a desert and they left the Flag."

From earth we prayed to heaven; being now
In heaven, we reverse the former prayer:
Earth of the cemeteries and cloudy seas,
Our small blue agate in the big black bag,
Earth mother of us, where we make our death,
Earth that the old man knocked on with his staff
Beseeching, "Leve moder, let me in,"

Hold us your voyagers safe in the hand
Of mathematics, grant us safe return
To where the food is, and the fertile dung,
To generation, death, decay; to war,
Gossip and beer, and bed whether warm or cold,
As from the heaven of technology
We take our dust and rocks and start back down.

HOWARD NEMEROV

THE DEPENDENCIES

This morning, between two branches of a tree
Beside the door, epeira once again
Has spun and signed his tapestry and trap.
I test his early-warning system and
It works, he scrambles forth in sable with
The yellow hieroglyph that no one knows
The meaning of. And I remember now
How yesterday at dusk the nighthawks came
Back as they do about this time each year,
Gray squadrons with the slashes white on wings
Cruising for bugs beneath the bellied cloud.
Now soon the monarchs will be drifting south,
And then the geese will go, and then one day
The little garden birds will not be here.
See how many leaves already have
Withered and turned; a few have fallen, too.
Change is continuous on the seamless web,
Yet moments come like this one, when you feel
Upon your heart a signal to attend
The definite announcement of an end
Where one thing ceases and another starts;
When like the spider waiting on the web
You know the intricate dependencies
Spreading in secret through the fabric vast
Of heaven and earth, sending their messages
Ciphered in chemistry to all the kinds,
The whisper down the bloodstream: it is time.

HOWARD NEMEROV

LATE SUMMER

Look up now at what's going on aloft—
Not in high heaven, only overhead,
Yet out of reach of, unaffected by,
The noise of history and the newsboy's cry.

There grow the globes of things to come,
There fruits and futures have begun to form
Solid and shadowy under the boughs:
Acorns in neat berets, horse chestnuts huge
And shiny as shoes inside their hedgehog husks,
Prickly planets among the sweetgum's starry leaves.

So secretly next year secretes itself
Within this one, as far on forested slopes
The trees continue quietly making news,
Enciphering in their potencies of pulp
The matrix of much that hasn't happened yet.

HOWARD NEMEROV

THE GUEST

Brother, I have wished you here to meet me
     where the lichened rocks
lead fifty yards into the sea, and vanish.
     Imagine old Homer
sitting on the last rock out, you say,
     a circle of stilled water
around his pale, puffed feet, remembering.
     Sandpipers skitter
past the carcass of a crab and the hard eye
     of a stiffened starfish,
their brittle legs quicker than foam. Homer does not
     distract them as they eat.
Tell me, brother, where do I go from here,
     what can I do?
Hatred cannot cure the emptiness
     that awaits us,
the blank light we live in. We cannot hate
     hatred away,
no cause is pure enough. It has been tried;
     over and over
the righteous have feasted on our blood.
     Homer's gods
have told him we are like the sea's own pulse,
     always changing,
remaining the same. I would accept that,
     but the threat
that always all that emptiness angers
     us to kill,
demands I will you to my side to tell me

it need not be so.
Pretend, you say, a sandpiper pursues
        another three times
around a boulder—a little Achilles,
        a little Hector;
they stop to poke for sand-crabs burrowing
        as the tide slips back,
alike on their locked legs, preening in the sun.
        Suddenly they spin
past staring Homer; he tightens, then
        reaches his hands out
pointing over the arching sea. What does he hear?
        I can see nothing
but the lane the sunlight makes—the lane
        you followed, brother,
as I wished you here to speak the wish
        I must devour
before I go. Embrace me. Touch my hair. Hold
        absolutely still.
If it is not too late to try again,
        say to me now
I may become the chosen laughter
        for your cause,
among those rocks, circled by sandpipers,
        with old Homer,
his loose feet chilled, his blank eyes feeling
        the salt in the air,
pointing forever over the sea.

ROBERT PACK

"THE MAN OF GRASS"

David Douglas, 1798-1834

1

I was David Douglas. I became a tree,
the fir, *pseudotsuga taxifolis.*
In 1825, one of Wordsworth's children,
I plunged through Oregon's woods "more like a man
Flying from something that he dreads than one
Who sought the thing he loved." What did I seek so long
in panic, out of mind of Scotland? Whom Nature
loves, like me, showing her eyes, goes far in dread—
I found and named my specimens of grass,
trees, vines, and ferns, like Adam
still taking dominion in a falling world.

2

Indians liked me, thought me mad like them. Once
beside Columbia I thrashed a grinning thief
and told them all, "I'm no blanket man or boston,
know me as the Man of Grass!" And having named
myself, strange phylum, wherever I might wander
in that green labyrinth the Indians greeted
me like a comic skookum, "Grass Man! Grass Man!"
They led me miles in search of giant pines
with nuts like sugar, so they promised, grinning.
Even so, limping into camp at night, I saw
their children run from me in terror. They were my mirror.

82

3

Along the Umpqua River in October
after a night of wind and lightning ravaging the trees
I found at last my Sugar Pine—Na-teel
the Umpquas call it. Who'd believe me, munching there
on nuts as sweet as toffee out of cones
the size of loaves? Alone, alone, bowing
to that grove of swaying towers. I felt
as though turning on the pin and center of my life.
Those great indifferent trees—how could I publish
to the sullen world what things alive they were?
Each was sacred quite without my worship, each
would one day crash to earth without my witness.
Beneath them, all I knew was punyness of knowledge,
the bitter joy of any thinking reed.

When I fired my piece to bring down cones (and aim myself)
the bushes filled with staring Indians stringing bows.
I quailed, and ran away, and hid myself all night
in a tangle of vines unknown to science. No one to tell.

4

Come day, I headed back to Fort Vancouver.
Then everywhere was back. I went back to Scotland
famous, to the Royal Society, to my family:
all nothing, dried specimens of another life.
I was good for nothing but to find new worlds, they joked,
and sent me out again, and indeed I ran
and ran those woods, collecting, classifying, naming
as before, but finding less and less beyond
the blow-down and grizzly thickets of my mind.

Finally, cruising the Sandwich Islands, I jumped
slow ship to walk the slopes of Mauna Kea.
There, in an earthen pit off-trail, a wild bull
was trapped and battering the sides, insane.
I leaned over and watched and watched—that brute
energy, baffled by walls of earth until
it choked, Nature blindly naturing, life from life,
indifference and fury . . . . When I had
it all in mind, when I'd told the suave Latin
of all my Oregon plants, when I'd seen
the grove of sugar pines clearly once again,
I, the Man of Grass, blessed the bull,
and slipped over the raw green edge, and in.

JAROLD RAMSEY

ANIMALS THAT DIE IN OUR HOUSES

A cat once walked off the roof into our garden
landing like a table on all fours.
We found a fieldmouse curled on linoleum
with paws drawn up
in an attitude of prayer.

In the clear balloon of the fishbowl
the goldfish make perfect breathy O's.
One fish, orange in the watery stratosphere
where the water is thin and dangerous,
floats upside down like a flag in distress.

Locked in that lunatic position,
the fish is a moon out of orbit,
out of grace with gravity; and, World,
has turned its back on you completely
and is wed to its new element, the sky.

What laws govern our houses,
our civilized many-roomed coffins above ground,
that invite these creatures to tunnel or chew
into our lives. Are ears and noses caves,
environments the insects find hospitable,

as in helicoptic circles they navigate
our sleeping heads. Is it accidental,
then, how they seem to swim closer to us in death,
or fall out of the sky like small
oddly-shaped chunks of heaven?

They occupy our lives so briefly,
the insect rocking in the bowl of its shell,
the fish pumped up to the water's breakable surface,
in death appear more innocent
than the shapes our minds invent.

Imposing on us, a kind of isolation,
they seem much more human than we are;
when, solitary and cautious, they watch us
lie in our formal positions
in the deep grass, in the woods, together.

JANE SHORE

·

MINING IN KILLDEER ALLEY

One a penny, two a penny, they settled in the driveway like
              flakes of air,
In the gravel halfway up the hill, their splayed toes mingling
With the generous shadows the grass tufts held,
                                    scratching softly
In the book of the guardians, you could say, as their crazed flight
Had mimed a calligraphy when they came down
From the fluent air to wobble on dumb straws
Like any stilted creature, off balance, hindered by strangeness.
The shadows were blue and voluminous, and their toes lost,
And the pronouns confused, and they staggered and took flight
Again as I drove over their place, and when I had entered the house
And called my wife to the window they were back, settled,
Settled into the dark; and in the morning of mountains
They parted, again, for my descent.
                              They were there
The last seven months before the gift,
Every day, flanking my passage
Like wings, their crooked wings, her shoulder blades
As she bent awkwardly before the sink, mornings, in the ninth month.

So that my father, who we thought was dying,
Could see him, we carried his grandson
Up the back stairs of the hospital. The light was broken
All over his blanket and our child swam in his glasses
With pieces of that broken light.
                         Their russet throats,
The sun shattered in the gravel,
                the gray veins
Of his impeccable wrist,
             Lord, for the life of me.

When we brought him home they had flown away.

DABNEY STUART

TOMORROW AND TOMORROW

Listening to the politicians of a spring evening
my mind veers and I am occupied
with the eggs of crickets warming
under last year's leaves;
I think on the cold sparked
intelligence of spiders
and how dragonflies make love,
two sets of wings in flight
a synchronized brightness of air.

Factual voices chat of treacheries deceit and death
but I hold to the notion of crickets unfolding
cell by cell into spring light,
the dragonflies floating in pairs
flashing like daggers in the warm air.
One must consider a spider's sense,
the precise bright thread of a spider's calculations.

LEE SUTTON

GLORY

Glory cried my red head, my sweet
    daughter,
Glory whispered she, mummy, he's a
    glorious creature.
Red his coat, fiery his temper,
Glory shall be the name of this fiery
    creature.

Wild from out the Outaouais woods
    came he,
Hungered, fierce, untamed but
    hawk-wounded,
Curious and ionized to her friendship free.
His wild, glorious pride she minded.

Come in Glory, she soothed, come to me
Kitty. He came, ate, slept, dust of God,
Bettered and gloriously into Sultan grew,
Got himself a harem, glorious he.

Brought his harem to the feeding bowls,
Sultannas, kittens and all.
Red their coats, red their tails,
Glories all these fiery creatures be.

JOSEPHINE HAMBLETON TESSIER

RESIDENTIAL HOTEL LOUNGE WITH TROPICAL FISH

In these tanks the ornamental fish,
Carnivores whom close-breeding's made effete,
Have all that they could wish, if they could wish.

The water is maintained at just the heat
Of those lagoons to which they are native and
Electrical tides ensure that it's kept sweet;

The bottom is strewn with bright and sifted sand
And miniature weeds in miniature currents sway.
All's here that fishy comfort could command;

The food comes regularly day by day,
The livestock takes no catching (being dead)
And no mouths lurk to which they might fall prey.

Such leisure breeds small frictions but the head
Of all their quarrels is but a swirl or eddy
(As is their courtship's climax if truth be said).

Outside the tank life here is quite as steady,
All its requirements noted and supplied
And someone always has the answers ready.

All know who smiled, who pouted and who sighed,
Whose complex is mere sex, whose guilt, whose fear.
No-one has anywhere he can really hide

To shed the public face or private tear.
Their hates, though bitter, come to petty issue,
Their loves, though passionate, are rather drear.

And all is held in an enclosing tissue
Frail as the glass in which the fish are cased,
And, like it, one sharp blow can cause the fissure

Through which their lives would spill. And the hand is raised.

W. M. Tidmarsh

TURNER IN OLD AGE

1

Remote, cantankerous and fat
little man, hermit-mossed and solitary,
he slipped all the hollow connections
his fame could have brought.

Odd shylock in retreat, his bleak ways
spread rumour of madness.
At Chelsea he locked his spirit
behind the screen of his landlady.

Praise was heaped, yet he festered
at those barbs of 'suds and whitewash,'
the dauber with a dripping brush
soaked in a bucket of ochre.

Puny man was swallowed by his canvas,
crumpling before nature, the brief split-
second of his span dissolving
against time, and its companion, light:

Yellow flame at morning, crimson
shockbursts of noon, an orange glow
sunk behind a ruined city;
rainbow shafts flooding through glass.

What he glimpsed was a passing
of empire, vainglorious shreds
at sunset, an edifice toppling
in broken masonry. The deluge.

Gondolas prowl through lagoons
between palaces that already sag,
their tapestry mildewed and flaked
like those ramshackle fallacies of hope.

2

Soured and gout-worn, he hid
from green calumny, dismayed by men,
by steam and speed slicing through nature.
Disgust drove him deeper into his hole.

It seemed as if life itself
was only a space to cram
the red and golden blaze of paint
across those distant horizons.

Like a haunting outside the frame
of day, the images from history
darken and clamp. For a moment the light
splinters, usurped by drumcloud.

Still he pieced that concept of something
lost and beyond us, a splash and streak
of sun and water fusing, the huge
melancholy of shaping a vision.

What it cost built his rack
and achievement, that stuns us now
as we look. An explosive mixing of pigments
made a radiance of mystery.

Down to the very end he sealed
his meaning: 'You cannot ever
read me, and do not care. Let it all
pass; go your ways.'

And then, as bent custom would have it,
they laid the painter in St. Paul's—
one skull that had seen the pure value of light,
the fleeting whirlwind of light . . .

JOHN TRIPP

HONORED GUEST*

"Earth receives an honored guest"
—Auden

Guest night. Breath-taking games and—spending.
I play hand-rubbing host, you guest condescending.

"Roll-call, roll-call, want to poll
Guest whims? Mine is: stretch and loll."

Can be arranged. First sign my scroll.
Ignore that digging. Just some mole.

"Is it to plant some tree, that hole?
To leap next May around a pole?"

There'll be no May, there'll be no leap.
Take three steps down to where you'll sleep.

"Umph, no big rush to get to bed.
That third step, why so red, so red?"

For honored guest, red carpets roll,
Inviting to a downward stroll.

"Who carved my name in stone above?
That second date—a 'date' with love?"

A hole you'll come for: hug so numbing
You'll lie there breathless. Till the Second Coming.

"Whose lucky name will roll-call call?
My heart skips like a roulette ball."

On guest night, gambling's not a sin;
Just say you bet your life you'll win.

"I'm a good egg—I'll close both eyes;
Now mix me up a real surprise."

Une omelette-surprise in a basement *boite*.
Good mixers fit so tight a spot.

    "I smell a rose—what ditch that closes
    Calls me to be smelled by roses?"

Today still munching bread on top.
Tomorrow pushing up the crop.

    "Night thickens round me like a bowl,
    And yet it's day. How almost droll!"

A condominium. Ask where-is-it,
And natives chuckle, 'You can't miss it.'

    "Roll-calls—like lizard tongues—unroll.
    Fat flies, not me, must be their goal."

Cashier is phoning change of role.
Call's collect, and you're the toll.

PETER VIERECK

* *"Charade: two speakers, alternating couplets. The couplets in quotes, indented throughout, are spoken (in pollyanna singsong) by 'you,' the honored mortal guest. The couplets without quotes are spoken by the obsequious host of a tourist resort."* —P.V.

WALKING AT NIGHT

After the sidewalk, after the last streetlight at the end
Of concrete crumbling into thickening weeds, I begin
Shuffling slowly off balance, my shadow's feet gone
    slipshod
Under mine, as it stretches further and further into the
    night,
Now spindly, fading to nothing as quickly as I darken.

I move, my legs more lost than in a swamp, going blind
Among the dead calm branches of a bush that knows
Where its thorns belong, blundering star-nosed as a mole
Through rubble, slanting and slumping, shortcutting
    myself
For no good reason: the last light shines where I
    abandoned it.

No wings, no antennae, no burning catch-all eyes, no
    echoes
Whistling back from the shapes out of my reach, no
    starlight
Scratching a line of march over the smudged heavens:
Nothing but streaks of cloud being rushed blue-gray as
    steel
Across the slammed vault of the sky, a moonless coffer,

Where the only guides are the heart in my mouth, my
    body's guesswork,
And sticks crackling under my feet as if in a dark fire.

                                   DAVID WAGONER

THE UNDOING

The old ice wears thin, thinner,
eroding to breakup. The rotten
lid of the pond quivers in gusts
as if bodies were rolling beneath it.
At the torn edge, a pure slit of light.

We scrawl KEEP OFF on a stick—
a warning to kids that the world will be water
by nightfall, the cattail margins mud
for the muskrat's feet.
                                     March again!
I am worn out already with process:

the shriek of frogs all night
in their scummy hollows,
their jellies, orgies, wars; the effort
of speech in a rising wind,
the effort of silence in birthing.

What secrets are left to rip open?
Out in the garden, winter's mulch
is needled to death in the morning rain,
already the weeds flex. Wherever we step
we sink in, moving through glacial ruts.

My love, I am not my own woman.
Today the wind walks through me
and over the field where last year's grasses
bend a little, and straighten again.
The old griefs recur, recur,

build and digest themselves like a soil,
like history—the bloodspot on the egg.
I no longer know what is mine or the world's.
I no longer know my sorrow in loving
from the sorrow of those I have loved.

KIM WALLER

ANSWER TO PRAYER

A Short Story That Could Be Longer

In that bad year, in a city to have now no name,
In the already-dark of a winter's day, our feet
Unsteady in slip-tilt and crunch of re-freezing snow as if lame,
And two hands ungloved to clasp closer though cold,
                                        down a side street

We moved. Ahead, intersecting, stretched the avenue where
Life clanged and flared like a gaudy disaster under
Whatever the high sky wombed in its dark imperative of air,
And where we, to meat and drink set, might soon pretend, or

At least hope, that sincerity could be bought by pain.
But now stopped. She said, "Wait!" And abrupt, was gone
Up the snow-smeared broad stone to dark doors before
                                        I could restrain

That sentimental idiocy. Alone,

As often before in a night-street, I raised eyes
To pierce what membrane remotely enclosed the great
                                bubble of light that now
The city inflated against the dark hover of infinities,
And saw how a first frail wavering stipple of shadow

Emerged high in that spectral concavity of light, and
                                drew down to be,
In the end, only snow. Then she, again there, to my
                                question, replied
That she had made a prayer. And I: "For what?" And she:
"Nothing much, just for you to be happy." Then cocking
                                her head to one side,

Looked up and grinned at me, an impudent eye-sparkling
                              grin, as though
She had just pulled the trick of the week, and on a cold-flushed
Cheek, at the edge of the grin for an accent, the single snow-
Flake settled, and gaily in insult she stuck her tongue
                              out, and blood rushed

To my heart. So with hands again nakedly clasped,
                              through the soft veil and swish
Of flakes falling, we moved toward the avenue. And
                              later, proceeded,
Beyond swirl and chain-clank of traffic, and a siren's far anguish,
To the unlit room to enact what comfort body and heart needed.

Who does not know the savvy insanity and wit
Of history! and how its most savage peripeteia always
Has the shape of a joke—if you find the heart to laugh at it.
In such a world, then, one must be pretty careful how he prays.

Her prayer, yes, was answered, for in spite of my meager desert,
Of a sudden, life—it was bingo! was bells and all ringing like mad,
Lights flashing, fruit spinning, the machine spurting
                              dollars like dirt—
Nevada dollars, that is—but all just a metaphor
                              for the luck I now had.

But that was long later, and as answer to prayer long out
Of phase. And now thinking of her, I can know neither
                              what, nor where,
She may be, and even in gratitude, I must doubt
That she ever remembers she ever prayed such a prayer.

Or remembering, she may laugh into the emptiness of air.

ROBERT PENN WARREN

ONE WAY TO LOVE GOD

Here is the shadow of truth, for only the shadow is true.
And the line where the incoming swell from the sunset Pacific
First leans and staggers to break tells all you need to know
About submarine geography, and your father's death rattle
Provides all biographical data required for the *Who's Who* of the dead.

I cannot recall what I started to tell you, but at least
I can say how night-long I have lain under stars and
Heard mountains moan in their sleep. By daylight
They remember nothing, and go about their lawful occasions
Of not going anywhere except in slow disintegration. At night
They remember, however, that there is something they cannot remember,
So moan. Theirs is the perfected pain of conscience, that
Of forgetting the crime, and I hope you have not suffered it. I have.

I do not recall what had burdened by tongue, but urge you
To think on the slug's white belly, how sick-slick and soft,
On the hairiness of stars, silver, silver, while the silence
Blows like wind by, and on the sea's virgin bosom unveiled
To give suck to the wavering serpent of the moon; and,
In the distance, in *plaza, place, piazza, platz,* and square,
Boot heels, like history being born, on cobbles bang.

Everything seems an echo of something else.

And when, by the hair, the headsman held up the head
Of Mary of Scots, the lips kept on moving,
But without sound. The lips,
They were trying to say something very important.

But I had forgotten to mention an upland
Of wind-tortured stone white in darkness, and tall, but when
No wind, mist gathers, and once on the Sarré at midnight,
I watched the sheep huddling. Their eyes
Stared into nothingness. In that mist-diffused light their eyes
Were stupid and round like the eyes of fat fish in muddy water,
Or of a scholar who has lost faith in his calling.

Their jaws did not move. Shreds
Of dry grass, gray in gray mist-light, hung
From the side of a jaw, unmoving.

You would think that nothing would ever again happen.

That is one way to love God.

ROBERT PENN WARREN

EVENING HAWK

From plane of light to plane, wings dipping through
Geometries and orchids that the sunset builds,
Out of the peak's black angularity of shadow, riding
The last tumultuous avalanche of
Light above pines and the guttural gorge,
The hawk comes.

          His wing
Scythes down another day, his motion
Is that of the honed steel-edge, we hear
The crashless fall of stalks of Time.

The head of each stalk is heavy with the gold of our error.

Look! look! he is climbing the last light
Who knows neither Time nor error, and under
Whose eye, unforgiving, the world, unforgiven, swings
Into shadow.

          Long now,
The last thrush is still, the last bat
Now cruises in his sharp hieroglyphics. His wisdom
Is ancient, too, and immense. The star
Is steady, like Plato, over the mountain.

If there were no wind we might, we think, hear
The earth grind on its axis, or history
Drip all night like a leaking pipe in the cellar.

ROBERT PENN WARREN

MIDNIGHT OUTCRY

Torn from the dream-life, torn from the life-dream,
Beside him in darkness, the cry bursts: *Oh!*
Endearment and protest—they avail
Nothing against whatever is so
Much deeper and darker than anything love may redeem.

He lies in the dark and tries to remember
How godlike to strive in passion and sweat,
But fears to awaken and clasp her, lest
Their whole life be lost, for he cannot forget
That the depths that cry rose from might shrivel a heart, or member.

How bright dawns morning!—how sweetly the face
Inclines over the infant to whom she gives suck.
So his heart leaps in joy, but remembering
That echo of fate beyond faith or luck,
He fixes his studious gaze on the scene to trace

In the least drop spilled between nipple and the ferocious
Little lip-suction, some logic, some white
Spore of the human condition that carries,
In whiteness, the dark need that only at night
Finds voice—but only and always one strange to us.

The day wore on; and he would ponder,
Lifting eyes from his work, thinking, thinking,
Of the terrible distance in love, and the pain,
Smiling back at the sunlit smile, though shrinking
At recall of the nocturnal timbre, and the dark wonder.

ROBERT PENN WARREN

ADDRESS TO EXISTENCE

While you are still in me
I am enabled to address you,
who, once you have laid me down,
shall be silent indeed—
for, though you have insisted on becoming me,
it is for a limited time only,
and now you are losing interest,
as you always eventually do,
taking up and, in the end, putting down, this one or that one,
be it man or beast, a Beethoven or an antelope.
Is diversity your purpose, I ask,
or is it that each and every thing must have its chance?
But you are indifferent to my questioning—
we are, at best, your puppets.
Nevertheless, there are moments when I seem to sense
a certain concern, a certain affection even, on your part:
by the way in which you keep my heart beating,
my body's defenses on the alert,
transmuting into my very self the food I eat,
doing for me, every day,
a thousand intricate and marvellous things,
of which I myself am totally incapable,
and so maintaining me as a conscious being.
How can I thank you for this,
for the grand experience of existing,
for remaining me, so many years—
you, who are upstream of language, of thought, of feeling even,
how could there be any way to thank you?
Yet I do thank you. I worship and adore you.
Before you leave me,
before I am no longer able to thank you,
I here do so, with all my heart.
And now lettest thou thy puppet lie down in peace.

JOHN HALL WHEELOCK

CLEF

His window overlooked birds.
Waking before them, he would count four bars
of introduction to their chorus with the useless
fingers of his left hand, rigid like boards.

All but severed by glass, their
flexibility gone, for two years now
he'd lived with them, inadequate as the loosened bow
clipped to his case lid; the violin's spare

strings close, but unable to
respond. Occasionally he would lift
the instrument out, hold it flat, admiring the cleft
wood figuring—the two mouths it sang through—

then lay unsubtle fingers
on its neck, roughly, as if to choke its
silence into renovating song. Love inhibits
violence and the harsh hand withdraws—strangers,

its fingers, to anger on
this feminine shape that gripped him early
with measured love—what he gave was given back truly
as his touch on wood was true. Now, to turn

from this mute interchange of
loss was hard; each time he would determine
to write letters, or read, there, curving in the margin,
before each line his eye would sketch a clef.

IVAN WHITE

A SKETCH

Into the lower right
Square of the window frame
There came
      with scalloped flight

A goldfinch, lit upon
The dead branch of a pine,
Shining,
      and then was gone,

Tossed in a double arc
Upward into the thatched
And crosshatched
      pine-needle dark.

Briefly, as fresh drafts stirred
The tree, he dulled and gleamed
And seemed
      more coal than bird,

Then, dodging down, returned
In a new light, his perch
A birch-
      twig, where he burned

In the sun's broadside ray,
Some seed pinched in his bill.
Yet still
            he did not stay,

But into a leaf-choked pane,
Changeful as even in heaven,
Even
            in Saturn's reign,

Tunnelled away and hid.
And then? But I cannot well
Tell you
            all that he did.

It was like glancing at rough
Sketches tacked on a wall,
And all
            so less than enough

Of gold on beaten wing,
I could not choose that one
Be done
            as the finished thing.

RICHARD WILBUR

CHILDREN OF DARKNESS

If groves are choirs and sanctuaried fanes,
What have we here?
An elm-bole cocks a bloody ear;
In the oak's shadow lies a strew of brains.
Wherever, after the deep rains,

The woodlands are morose and reek of punk,
These gobbets grow—
Tongue, lobe, hand, hoof, or butchered toe
Amassing on the fallen branch half-sunk
In leaf-mold, or the riddled trunk.

Such violence done, it comes as no surprise
To notice next
How some, parodically sexed,
Puff, blush, or gape, while shameless phalloi rise,
To whose slimed heads come carrion flies.

Their gift is not for life, these creatures who
Disdain to root,
Will bear no stem or leaf, no fruit,
And, mimicking the forms which they eschew,
Make it their pleasure to undo

All that has heart and fibre. Yet of course
What these break down
Wells up refreshed in branch and crown.
May we not after all forget that Norse
Drivel of Wotan's panicked horse,

And every rumor bred of forest-fear?
Are these the brood
Of adders? Are they devil's food,
Minced witches, or the seed of rutting deer?
Nowhere does water stand so clear

As in stalked cups where pine has come to grief;
The chanterelle
And cepe are not the fare of hell;
Where coral schools the beech and aspen leaf
To seethe like fishes of a reef,

Light strikes into a gloom in which are found
Red disc, gray mist,
Gold-auburn firfoot, amethyst,
Food for the eye whose pleasant stinks abound,
And dead men's fingers break the ground.

Gargoyles is what they are at worst, and should
They preen themselves
On being demons, ghouls, or elves,
The holy chiaroscuro of the wood
Still would embrace them. They are good.

RICHARD WILBUR

IN LIMBO

What rattles in the dark? The blinds at Brewster?
I am a boy then, sleeping by the sea,
Unless that clank and chittering proceed
From a bent fan blade somewhere in the room,
The air-conditioner of some hotel
To which I came too deadbeat to remember.
Let me, in any case, forget and sleep.
But listen: under my billet window, grinding
Through the shocked night of France, I surely hear
A convoy moving up, whose treads and wheels
Trouble the planking of a wooden bridge.

For a half-kindled mind that flares and sinks,
Damped by a slumber which may be a child's,
How to know when one is, or where? Just now
The hinged roof of the Cinema Vascello
Smokily opens, beaming to the stars
Crashed majors of a final panorama,
Or else that spume of music, wafted back
Like a girl's scarf or laughter, reaches me
In adolescence and the Jersey night,
Where a late car, tuned in to wild casinos,
Guns past the quiet house toward my desire.

Now I could dream that all my selves and ages,
Pretenders to the shadowed face I wear,
Might, in this clearing of the wits, forgetting
Deaths and successions, parley and atone.
It is my voice which prays it; mine replies
With stammered passion or the speaker's pause,

Rough banter, slogans, timid questionings—
Oh, all my broken dialects together;
And that slow tongue which mumbles to invent
The language of the mended soul is breathless,
Hearing an infant howl demand the world.

Someone is breathing. Is it I? Or is it
Darkness conspiring in the nursery corner?
Is there another lying here beside me?
Have I a cherished wife of thirty years?
Far overhead, a long susurrus, twisting
Clockwise or counterclockwise, plunges east—
Twin floods of air in which our flagellate cries,
Rising from love-bed, childbed, bed of death,
Swim toward recurrent day. And farther still,
Couched in the void, I hear what I have heard of,
The god who dreams us, breathing out and in.

Out of all that I fumble for the lamp chain,
A room condenses and at once is true—
Curtains, a clock, a mirror which will frame
This blinking mask the light has clapped upon me.
How quickly, when we choose to live again,
As Er once told, the cloudier knowledge passes!
I am a truant portion of the all
Misshaped by time, incorrigible desire,
And dear attachment to a sleeping hand,
Who lie here on a certain day and listen
To the first birdsong, homelessly at home.

RICHARD WILBUR

TWELVE RIFFS FOR YUSEF LATEEF

1

A negro sits in a yellow room in San Francisco
blowing an oboe.

2

A negro playing an alto sax in a room
freshly dusted with yellow pollen
draws the mountains closer to the city.
The mountains arrive wearing poppies in their hair
and clasps of wild bees.

3

An ebony face set off by a yellow room
and oboe music wilder than Bedouin bagpipes
turn the city into Solomon's halls.

4

Yusef Lateef has honey in his teeth
and his tongue is a honey cake
and his oboe is carved from the cedars of Lebanon
and he sits in a yellow honeycomb room
building sweet cells.

5

Be, black man, the god of light.
Step out of your yellow cave
and clatter your hooves on the pavement.
Charm us out of our gray flannel skins.
O your flute is a flowering branch,
a wand, a cornucopia.
All the Muni busses will form a chain
and follow you into the sunset
honking wildly.

6

The city shifts its icy shelves
and grates another inch towards the sea.
In the following silence
the bars of oboe music floating
from a room of yellow ice
are as plaintive as a loon's cry.

7

Oboe negro. The blues. Dark Jamaica rum.
Dark bodies pressed together in slave ships,
their bruises oozing like molasses.
Dark bodies moaning in the cypresses.
Dark fruit dripping in the poplars.
Scent of magnolia, obscene scent of magnolia.
Dark musician in a violent yellow room
slip your oboe between our ribs
and tell us of the negro darkness.

8

The Pacific listens. The waves,
like plates of Spanish armor, lean forward to hear;
Vasco Nuñez de Balboa, poised on a cresting cliff,
lifts off his helmet to listen;
Montezuma's aviaries hush their twittering to listen;
a Sioux, sounding the dark Plains night,
stops his flageolet to listen;
a calliope player in Whitman's Mannahatta
detects an unusual timbre in the air
and pauses to listen;
the dance halls on the Barbary Coast go dark
and the silent pianos listen—
to a negro in a yellow room
who has carved an oboe from their throats.

9

A black musician in a yellow room
questions the cigarette pastorals,

the Salem landscapes where everyone's chic
and the only suffering is over an empty pack.
The pitch of his oboe says
that many cut their wrists by the purling waters;
that suddenly the scene may darken
and the American night
cover us like a cop's black leather jacket.

10

We live in cacophonous cities
where lives are swept under
by grating waves of noise:
hosts of bulldozers blade up the silence;
loud dogs jar sleep,
hurtling at houses like derailed cable cars.
And we like it. We feed on it.
We turn up the volume.
Our ears have grown callouses
tougher than barnacles.
We do not hear the dark player
in a yellow room
who holds the planet in his cupped hands
like a Chinese globular flute.

11

The American day topples on us
like a crumbling freeway
and we are pinned beneath slabs
of gray light,
each of us jacknifed on himself.
Rescue us, Yusef,
from the harsh music
of sirens and suicides.

12

O black poet sequestered in a yellow room
the landscape is desperate for the spirit of music.

WILLIAM WITHERUP

THE PAINTER

I want a strong figure in the foreground,
a woman with large hips
balancing on a wooden chair
on one thigh
in an empty room.
Her body is the rhythm; she's jazzy.
Her arms, a pair, white,
run down her sides
like milk, form a river.
Toes swim.
You must imagine
the river: she is in an empty room.

Due to the stubborn streak I worked
into her cheekbones,
she will not appreciate her advantage.
She feels unfinished,
wants more than I give.
Tell her, she will always be beautiful.
Fluidity: aftermath of movement,
she surpasses all I have done to her.
I laugh as I tell you this:
she's been in control from the first.

Do not confuse this woman with me.
She is much stronger.
I make her the wrong colors,
disproportionate and precariously
balanced, to assert myself.
She fears nothing, stares
at my blundering hands.

I didn't tell you, she has eyes
like black pearls, like mine.
Her belly is brown and full, starving,
resembling the sum of my experiences.
When I move, I leave no forwarding address;
then she shows up in her empty room.
She's the lover I never
satisfy. She wants to drown me
in the river between us.

ELLEN WITTLINGER

THE FIVE DREAMS

What are the five dreams of the elders?

Richard, for all his beard, has seen
mist on an autumn pond and hears
water, the color of cognac, rising
and falling in the reeds of the shallows.
He thrusts his fingers through his hair
and each nail glistens with oil.
He knows that water is giving and taking,
and that it will give and take though fists
slam shut, though the high curse
of his name burns on the door plate.

Wayne is backed against a wall of books,
and the fireplace, the *place* of fire,
reddens his forehead. In his nostrils,
two cables of air freeze, and on them
he hangs in the world. He spreads his arms,
one hand the wing of a leather testament;
the other, the one with a dead ring,
seizes a last book of poetry.
The fire eats all shadows but one.

These were two dreams of the elders.

Emily has brushed her hair forever.
Now it is earth, and pours to her feet.
Half moons glint at her fingertips,
and sand drifts from her mouth, her ears,
the corners of her eyes. She is content.
It was prophesied. Her children look in
at the windows, pale as moonlight.

Remember when they gnawed her breasts?
When she is empty, they will press her
in a book, the book of earth.

Mary knows there are dead places in her.
The doctors, well, the doctors are guessing.
Richard's kiss is dead, but we all
shed layers, and when we have been struck
too often, part of us turns to the wall.
She knows, too, that when the last cobs
of snow melt, green incoherence leaps
from eye to eye. And Wayne's ring?
Well, it turned green before it died.
She takes it off. It pings on the parquet.
The ring scar reddens. She feels better.

This is the last dream of the elders.

Each house has a room that's always locked.
This is the room of dreaming. Sometimes
it is a room of water where a huge eye
glares. Sometimes there is a bed
of glacial sheets, slow, slow, and in them
we can see our gill parents. And, praise God,
one night the young of us will lie down together
in a shadow of black hair. And one day
we will return, put down our cases,
pass through the room where the fist
opens, where the earth sifts, where the ring
spins to quiet. Then, we lie down in the milky,
slow sheets, when the door closes
and is a door no longer.

JOHN WOODS

LYING DOWN WITH MEN AND WOMEN

When we came up from water, our eyes
drew to the front of our heads,
and we had faces. When we came up
on our knuckles, we held fruit to our mouths,
and wanted to know the chemistry
of sweetness.
                    Then as we walked down
the earth's curve, trees and hills
got in our way, so we moved them
for roads and newsprint and wreckage.

Part of every day, the water mood and the tree mood
rise in our bodies, and we must
lie down a bit to honor our lost
tails and gills.
                    When we lie on our backs,
we see so far away we try to give names to light,
like wild dogs we have taught
to lick our hands.
                    And when we lie on our faces,
we see too close, the blank wall
at the end of the corridor.
                                        And so

we lie down with men and women
because we are terrified, and sometimes,
for that reason, we stand up and kill.

                    JOHN WOODS

HOOK

I was only a young man
In those days. On that evening
The cold was so God damned
Bitter there was nothing.
Nothing. I was in trouble
With a woman, and there was
Nothing there but
Me and dead snow.

I stood on the streetcorner
In Minneapolis, lashed
This way and that.
Wind rose from some pit,
Hunting me.
Another bus to Saint Paul
Would arrive in three hours,
If I was lucky.
Oh, I am plenty lucky.

Then the young Sioux
Loomed beside me, his scars
Were just my age.

Ain't got no bus here
A long time, he said.
You got enough money
To get home on?

What did they do
To your hand? I answered.
He raised up his hook into the terrible starlight
And slashed the wind.

Oh, that? he said.
I had a bad time with a woman. Here,
You take this.

Did you ever feel a man hold
Sixty-five cents
In a hook,
And place it
Gently
In your freezing hand?

I took it.
It wasn't the money I needed.
But I took it.

JAMES WRIGHT